Searchlight BOOKS™

How Do Simple Machines Work?

Put Wheels and Axles to the Test

Sally M. Walker and Roseann Feldmann

Lerner Publications Company
Minneapolis

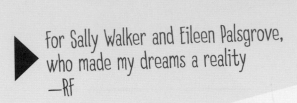

For Sally Walker and Eileen Palsgrove,
who made my dreams a reality
—RF

Lerner Publications Company
A division of Lerner Publishing Group, Inc.
241 First Avenue North
Minneapolis, MN 55401 U.S.A.

Website address: www.lernerbooks.com

Library of Congress Cataloging-in-Publication Data

Walker, Sally M.
        Put wheels and axles to the test / by Sally M. Walker and Roseann Feldmann.
            p.   cm. — (Searchlight books™—How do simple machines work?)
        Includes index.
        ISBN 978–0–7613–5326–3 (lib. bdg. : alk. paper)
        1. Wheels—Juvenile literature. 2. Axles—Juvenile literature. I. Feldmann, Roseann.
    II. Title.
    TJ181.5.W36 2012
    621.8078—dc22   2010029108

Manufactured in the United States of America
1 – DP – 7/15/11

Contents

Chapter 1

WORK

You work every day. At home, one of your chores may be doing dishes. At school, you work when you sharpen your pencil.

You work at snack time. And you work when you race in gym. Eating and playing are work too!

Playing soccer is work! What does the word *work* mean to a scientist?

Work = Using Force to Move an Object

When scientists use the word *work*, they don't mean the opposite of play. Work is using force to move an object. Force is a push or a pull. You use force to do chores, to play, and to eat.

You do work when you put newspapers into the recycling bin.

Anytime you use force to move an object to a new place, you have done work. Maybe the object moves hundreds of feet. Or maybe it moves only a tiny bit.

Riding a bike is work. Your force makes the bike's pedals turn. This makes you move forward.

You use force when you push your friend on a swing.

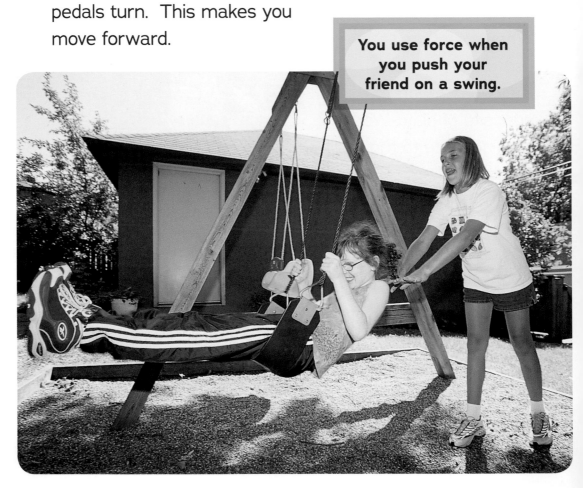

Pushing a Building Is NOT Work!

Pushing a school building is not work. It's not work even if you sweat. No matter how hard you try, you haven't done work. The building hasn't moved. If the building moves, then you have done work!

These kids are pushing very hard on a school building. But they are not doing work.

Chapter 2
MACHINES

Most people want to make their work easy. Machines are tools that make work easier. Some machines make work go faster too.

Trains have many moving parts. What are machines that have many moving parts called?

Complicated and Simple Machines

Some machines have many moving parts. They are complicated machines. Trains and cars are complicated machines.

Some machines have few moving parts. These machines are called simple machines. Simple machines are found in every home, school, and playground. These machines are so simple that most people don't realize they are machines.

The wheels on this chair are simple machines.

Chapter 3

FRICTION

Lay a book flat on a table. Give the book a push. It's easy to make the book slide a few inches. But you can make it even easier.

It is easy to make a book slide on a table. How can you make this even easier?

YOU'LL NEED THE BOOK, A ROUND
PENCIL, A STRAW, A SHEET OF
PAPER, AND A SPOOL.

▼

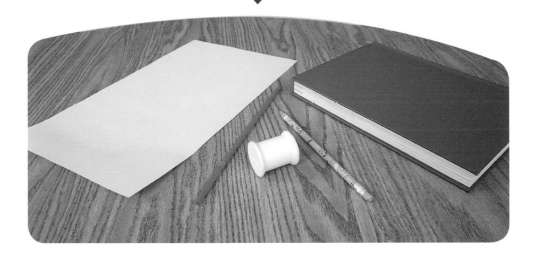

What You Do

Put the round pencil under the book. Push the book
again. A tiny push makes the book move easily. The
pencil made your work easier. You used the pencil as a
simple machine.

It is easier to push the book with a pencil under it.

How Does It Work?

It is easy to push the book when it lies flat on the table.
But it is even easier to push the book with a pencil
under it. This is because there is friction between the
book and the tabletop. Friction is a force that makes a
moving object slow down or stop. When the book is flat
on the table, its whole side touches the table. The book
slides only if your pushing force is stronger than friction's
stopping force.

Look at the book while the pencil is under it. The pencil lifts the book above the table. Only one edge of the book touches the table. So there is almost no friction between the book and the table. That's why you don't have to push as hard. But there is still some friction. Where do you think there is still friction?

The pencil lifts most of the book above the table. So there is very little friction between the book and the table.

Finding Friction

Take the book off the pencil. Look at the pencil. Part of the pencil touches the table. There's friction where the table and the pencil touch. You can prove it.

There is friction where the table and the pencil touch.

Put a sheet of paper on the table. Put the pencil at one end of the paper. Push the pencil. What happens? It rolls. But then it stops. Friction makes the pencil stop. Try the same thing with the straw. The straw also rolls until friction stops it.

Friction makes the pencil stop rolling.

Pretend there is no friction between the straw and the table. Then the straw would never stop rolling. What could you do to make less friction between the table and the straw?

Making Less Friction

Put your straw at one end of the paper. Draw a line right in front of the straw. Then roll the straw again. When the straw stops moving, pick it up. Put the pencil in its place. The pencil marks the straw's finish line.

Draw a line in front of the straw.

You can lower the friction between the straw and the table. Slide the spool onto the straw. Now only the spool's narrow edges touch the table. Start from the same line you drew in front of the straw before. Push the spool and the straw. Try to use the same amount of force as you did before.

What happens? The spool and the straw roll farther together than the straw rolled alone.

The spool and the straw roll with enough force to push the pencil.

Chapter 4

PARTS OF A WHEEL AND AXLE

When you put a spool on a straw, you make a simple machine. It is called a wheel and axle. An axle goes through the center of a wheel. Your spool is a wheel. Your straw is an axle. The straw goes through the center of the spool.

When the spool and the straw are together, they are a simple machine. What is this machine called?

Different Kinds of Wheels and Axles

Sometimes people use a wheel that spins around an axle. Hold your straw so it can't turn. Push the spool. The spool spins around the straw.

Try drawing a line around the spool. This will help you to see the spool spin.

YOU'LL NEED A SPOOL, A BOOK,
PAPER, A STRAW, AND A THICK
PENCIL FOR THE NEXT EXPERIMENT.

Sometimes people use a wheel and an axle that turn together. Take the spool off the straw. Put the spool on a thick pencil. It is all right if the spool only fits on the sharpened end of the pencil.

This time, your pencil is the axle. The axle fits tightly into the wheel's center. You can't turn the wheel without turning the axle.

The spool should fit tightly on the pencil. If your pencil is too thin, wrap some masking tape around it to make it thicker.

Wheels and Axles All Around

Look at the wheel and axle made by the spool and the pencil. It looks like a screwdriver. A screwdriver is a wheel and axle. Its thick handle and thin metal shaft turn together to screw in a screw.

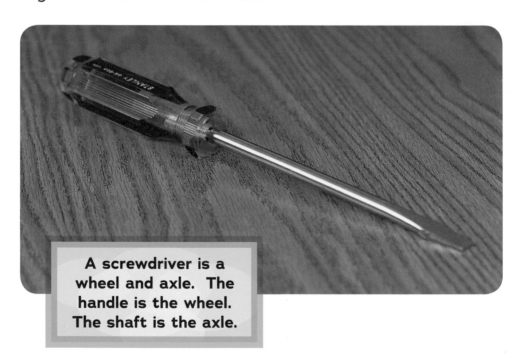

A screwdriver is a wheel and axle. The handle is the wheel. The shaft is the axle.

A doorknob is also a wheel and axle. The doorknob is the wheel. You can't see the axle. The axle is inside the door. The doorknob and its axle turn together. When you turn the knob, it moves other parts inside the door. When those parts move, the door opens.

Faucet handles are wheels. When you turn the handles, other parts inside the faucet move. Then water flows.

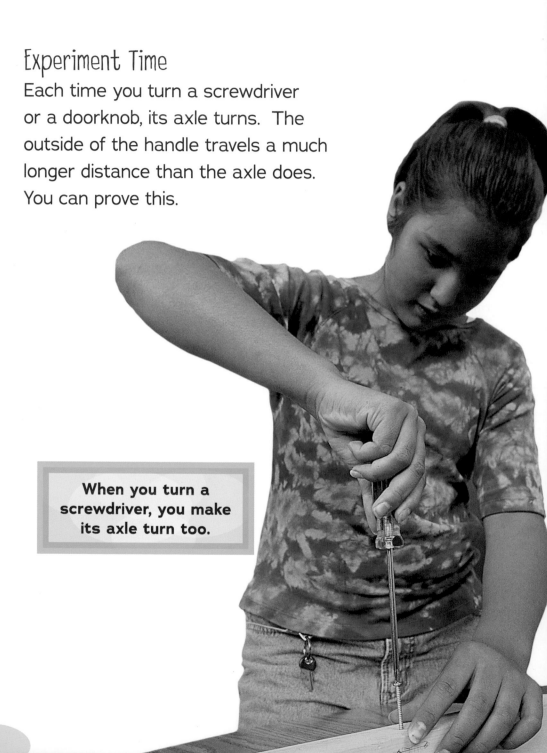

Experiment Time

Each time you turn a screwdriver or a doorknob, its axle turns. The outside of the handle travels a much longer distance than the axle does. You can prove this.

When you turn a screwdriver, you make its axle turn too.

Pull the pencil out of the spool. Draw a dot on the spool's edge. Then draw a dot on a sheet of paper. Line up the two dots. Slowly roll the spool until its dot touches the paper again. Mark the paper with another dot. The distance between the two dots on the paper is equal to one full turn of the spool. The wheel rolls a long distance in one turn.

Slowly roll the spool until the dot touches the paper again.

Now make a dot on the side of your pencil. Line it up with the first dot on the paper. Slowly roll the pencil until its dot touches the paper again. Mark the paper with another dot.

Make a dot on the side of the pencil. You can use chalk, a pen, or a marker.

You can see that one turn of the pencil is a shorter distance than one turn of the spool. Remember, the pencil is the axle and the spool is the wheel. So one turn of the axle is shorter than one turn of the wheel.

Turning a large wheel is easier than turning a small axle. So your work is easier. You can prove this.

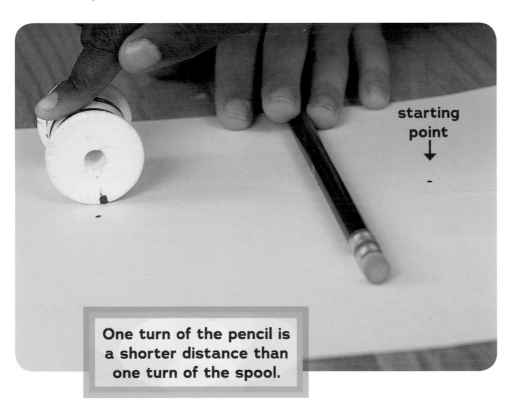

starting point

One turn of the pencil is a shorter distance than one turn of the spool.

Try turning an axle instead of its wheel. It takes more force to do your work that way.

Now Try This!

Get a screwdriver. Ask an adult to find a screw for you to turn. Hold the screwdriver's thin shaft. Try to unscrew the screw. It is hard to do. You must use a lot of force.

Try it again. But this time, hold the handle of the screwdriver. It is probably easy to turn the screw. You turn the wheel a longer distance than you turned the shaft. But you don't have to use as much force. That makes your work easier.

It is easier to turn a wheel a long distance than it is to turn its axle a short distance.

Unicycles, Bicycles, and Tricycles

Sometimes one wheel and its axle are all you need to do work. A unicycle has one wheel and axle. Riding a unicycle is fun. But balancing on it is hard. The rider can tip over easily.

Sometimes it helps to add more wheels and axles. Two wheels make balancing easier. But learning to ride a bike with two wheels is still hard. The bike tips over if you stop moving.

A unicycle has just one wheel and axle.

A tricycle is easy to ride. It has two back wheels. These wheels share one axle. A tricycle also has a front wheel and axle. These three wheels make a tricycle steady.

Wagons

It's very easy to ride in a wagon. A wagon has two axles and four wheels. The four wheels make the wagon very steady. You have to work hard to tip over a wagon.

A tricycle has two back wheels and one front wheel. A wagon has four wheels. Riders don't have to balance on tricycles or wagons.

Chapter 5

GEARS

Some wheels are smooth. Other wheels have teeth. What are wheels with teeth called?

Wheels and axles are many sizes and shapes. Some wheels are big. Others are small. Some axles are long. Others are short. Different wheels and axles are used for different jobs. Some wheels have teeth. Teeth are bumps around the edge of a wheel. A wheel with teeth is called a gear.

Gears Work Together

Two gears work together. The teeth of one gear fit between the teeth of the other gear. When one gear turns, its teeth push against the teeth of the other gear. So the other gear turns too!

What do you think will happen if someone turns the green gear?

Turning the green gear makes the red gear turn too. But the red gear turns in the opposite direction from the way the green gear turns.

Look at a can opener. Squeeze the handles together. Notice how one gear's teeth fit into the spaces between the other gear's teeth. The knob is attached to one of the gears. Turn the knob. This action turns both gears. But the gears move in opposite directions.

When you turn the handle of a can opener, the gears turn in opposite directions.

Bicycle Gears

Sometimes gears work together even though they do not touch each other. Look at the big gear near a bike's pedals. It is far away from the small gear in the back wheel. But a chain wraps around both gears. The teeth of the gears poke into the links of the chain. The chain connects the gears.

A bike has a large gear near the pedals and a small gear in the back wheel.

A bike's pedal is a big handle. The pedal turns the big gear. When the big gear turns, the chain moves with it. The links of the chain are hooked on the teeth of the small gear. When the chain moves, the small gear turns. When the small gear turns, the back wheel of the bike turns. Maybe it turns fast enough for you to win a race!

The pedals turn the big gear.
The big gear turns the chain.
The chain turns the small gear.
Then the back wheel turns.

You have learned a lot about wheels and axles. Using a wheel gives you an advantage. An advantage is a better chance of finishing your work. Using a wheel and axle is almost like having a helper. That means you'll have time to do more work, like skating!

Wheels and axles make work easier!

Glossary

axle: a bar that goes through the center of a wheel

complicated machine: a machine that has many moving parts

force: a push or a pull

friction: a force caused when two objects rub together

gear: a wheel with bumps around its edge

simple machine: a machine that has few moving parts

wheel: a round object that turns on an axle

work: moving an object from one place to another